Brook Meets Farook!

Written by Dan White

Illustrated by Rocky Leaw

Brook was waiting at the hospital.

I am Brook!
I am Farook!
We are Mr and Mrs Hosein.

Farook had hurt his leg.
How did it get like that?
I fell over playing in a match. It hurt so much! Now I am getting a wheelchair, just like you.

What is it like to be in a wheelchair?
It is my transport.

HOSPITAL EXIT
Soon Farook had his wheels ...

... but he felt upset.

I cannot play or have fun!
Can you explain?

I cannot run fast
in a wheelchair.

I cannot play games
with my pals. They will
have fun and I will not.

I cannot swim –
I need this chair.

Brook made a plan. She needed to
let Farook see all the fun she had.

You can still have
fun in a wheelchair.
How?

You can zoom like this.
Wow! This is faster than running!

You can still play games.
Woo-hoo!

You can swim.

Brook, you are the best!

Farook's leg was soon better.
Shall we go and play in the park?
I bet I can get there quicker than you!